EXPLORING CONTINENTS

SOUTH AMERICA

Anita Ganeri

Heinemann LIBRARY

H www.heinemann.co.uk/library
Visit our website to find out more information about Heinemann Library books.

J918 / 4148335

Leabharlann Contae na Mídhe

To order:
☎ Phone 44 (0) 1865 888066
🖹 Send a fax to 44 (0) 1865 314091
🖳 Visit the Heinemann Bookshop at www.heinemann.co.uk/library to browse our catalogue and order online.

First published in Great Britain by Heinemann, Halley Court, Jordan Hill, Oxford, OX2 8EJ, part of Harcourt Education.

Editorial: Louise Galpine and Harriet Milles
Design: Richard Parker and Q2A Solutions
Illustrations: Jeff Edwards
Picture Research: Mica Brancic and Beatrice Ray
Production: Camilla Crask

Originated by Chroma
Printed and bound in China by WKT

10 digit ISBN 0 431 09748 8 (hardback)
13 digit ISBN 978 0 431 09748 0 (hardback)

11 10 09 08 07
10 9 8 7 6 5 4 3 2 1

British Library Cataloguing in Publication Data
Ganeri, Anita
  South America. - (Exploring continents)
  1.South America - Geography - Juvenile literature
  I.Title
  918
A full catalogue record for this book is available from the British Library.

Acknowledgements
Alamy pp. **9** (Blickwinkel), **10** (David Noton), **13** (A Parada), **15** (Thomas Shjarback); Bridgeman Art Library p. **20**; Corbis pp. **17** (Ann Johansson), **22** (Alison Wright), **24**, **27** (Richard T Nowitz); Getty pp. **7** (Stone), **8** (Image Bank), **11** (Photographers choice), **14** (National Geographic), **21** (Stone), **25** (Aurora), **26** (Taxi); Lonely Planet pp. **5** (Jeff Greenberg), **23** (Richard I'Anson); Travel Ink p. **18**.

Cover satellite image of South America reproduced with permission of SPL/M-Sat Ltd.

Every effort has been made to contact copyright holders of any material reproduced in this book. Any omissions will be rectified in subsequent printings if notice is given to the publishers.

CONTENTS

Words that appear in the text in bold, **like this**, are explained in the Glossary.

WHAT IS A CONTINENT?

About two-thirds of the Earth is covered in water. The rest of the Earth is made up of seven huge pieces of land, called continents. Each of the continents, apart from Antarctica, is divided up into smaller regions called countries. This book is about the continent of South America.

How big is South America?

South America is the fourth largest continent in the world. It covers about 12 per cent of the Earth's land surface. It stretches from the countries of Colombia and Venezuela in the north to Cape Horn (part of Chile) in the far south.

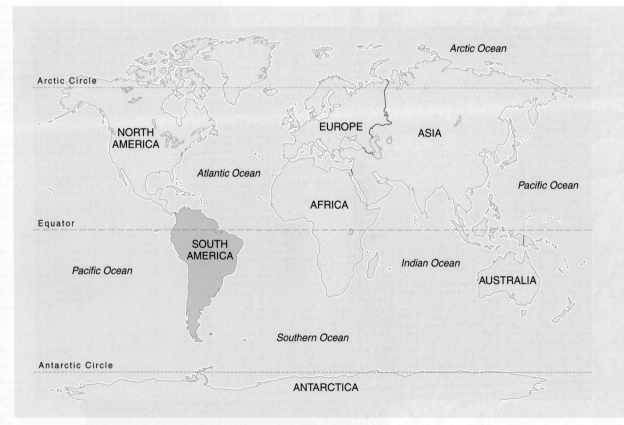

This map shows the seven continents of the world.

The Caribbean Sea lies to the north, the Pacific Ocean to the west, and the Atlantic Ocean to the east. To the south, a narrow stretch of water called the Drake Passage separates South America from Antarctica. To the north, the continent is connected to Central America by a long, narrow strip of land, called the **Isthmus** of Panama.

South American islands

South America has several groups of islands. The largest group is Tierra del Fuego, off the southern tip of the continent. These rocky, windswept islands are shared between Argentina and Chile. The Galapagos Islands lie about 1,000 kilometres (600 miles) off the west coast of Ecuador.

The Galapagos Islands are famous for their unusual wildlife, including giant tortoises.

WHAT DOES SOUTH AMERICA LOOK LIKE?

The landscape of South America is amazingly varied. There are enormous plains called grasslands, towering mountains, raging rivers, and vast tropical rainforests.

Tropical rainforests

Tropical rainforests cover over a third of South America. The largest is the Amazon rainforest which grows mostly in Brazil. It is the largest tropical rainforest on Earth. It covers more than 5 million square kilometres (2 million square miles), an area almost the size of Australia. Smaller patches of rainforest grow along the northwest and northeast coasts. The forests are rich in wildlife.

This map shows the different kinds of landscape found across the continent of South America.

Lake Maracaibo
R. Orinoco
Angel Falls
Guiana Highlands
North Atlantic Ocean
Equator
Galapagos Islands
Andes
R. Amazon
R. Madeira
R. Araguaia
Brazilian Highlands
Lake Titicaca
Mato Grosso Plateau
Atacama Desert
Gran Chaco
Iguazu Falls
R. Paraná
Pacific Ocean
Pampas
Patagonia
N
W E
S
South Atlantic Ocean
Falkland Islands
0   800 miles
0   1000 km
South Georgia

The Amazon River is so large that it can be clearly seen from space.

Rivers

The Amazon River is the longest river in South America and the second longest in the world. It begins in the Andes Mountains in Peru. Then it flows for 6,400 kilometres (4,000 miles) across Peru and Brazil to the Atlantic Ocean. The Amazon carries more water than any other river on Earth. Other important rivers in South America include the Orinoco, Parana, and São Francisco.

Great grasslands

Grasslands are huge, open plains that cover over half of South America. In Argentina, they are called the **pampas**. Large parts of the pampas are used for raising cattle for beef. Other parts are used for growing crops, such as wheat, **maize**, and beans. Another vast region of grassland lies in Colombia and Venezuela. These plains are called *llanos*.

Lakes

The biggest lake in South America is Lake Maracaibo in Venezuela, at 13,512 square kilometres (5,217 square miles). Valuable supplies of oil have been discovered underneath the lake. Lake Titicaca lies high up in the Andes Mountains on the border of Peru and Bolivia. At 3,810 metres (12,500 feet) above sea level, it is the highest lake that boats can sail on. Local people use reeds growing around the lake shore to make huts and fishing boats.

Angel Falls in Venezuela is the world's highest waterfall. Here, the River Churún plunges 979 metres (3,212 feet) down the side of a cliff called Devil's Mountain. The falls were named after American pilot, Jimmy Angel, who flew over them in 1935.

Many of the peaks in the Andes are over 6,000 metres (19,685 feet) high.

Mighty mountains

The Andes are the longest mountain range in the world. They stretch for 7,250 kilometres (4,504 miles) along the west coast of South America. The Andes were formed millions of years ago by movements of the Earth's **crust**. These movements are still happening, causing earthquakes and volcanic **eruptions** across the region.

The two mountainous regions in the east are called the Guiana Highlands and the Brazilian Highlands. Here, the peaks are lower and more rounded than the Andes. The highest mountain in this area is Pico da Bandeira in Brazil, at 2,890 metres (9,482 feet) tall.

LANDSCAPE FACTS

Highest mountain: Aconcagua, Argentina – 6,959 m (22,834 ft)

Lowest point: Valdes Peninsula, Argentina – 40 m (131 ft) below sea level

Longest river: Amazon River – 6,400 km (4,000 miles)

Largest lake: Lake Maracaibo, Venezuela – 13,512 sq km (5,217 sq miles)

Highest waterfall: Angel Falls, Venezuela – 979 m (3,212 ft)

Biggest desert: Patagonian, Argentina – 673,000 sq km (260,000 sq miles)

Largest forest: Amazon rainforest – 5 million sq km (2 million sq miles)

Biggest island: Tierra del Fuego – 47,000 sq km (18,100 sq miles)

WHAT IS THE WEATHER LIKE IN SOUTH AMERICA?

South America has a wide variety of different **climates**. They range from steamy tropical rainforests, to bone-dry deserts, to icy cold mountain glaciers.

Hot and cold

Most of South America has warm weather all year round. This is because much of the land lies around the **equator**. The hottest weather is in the Gran Chaco, a huge, dry plain in northern Argentina. Here, temperatures can reach a scorching 43°C (109°F). The south of the continent has cooler winters than the north. Chilly winds from Antarctica may bring snow and cold weather. This can cause winter temperatures in the far south of Argentina and Chile to fall to minus 33°C (minus 27.4°F).

The Perito Moreno Glacier is one of the coldest places in Patagonia, Argentina.

In some parts of the Atacama Desert, no rain has ever been recorded.

Wet and dry

Most places in South America have regular rainfall. The wettest place is Quibdo in Colombia with more than 8,900 mm (350 inches) of rain a year. By contrast, the Atacama Desert is one of the driest places on Earth. It stretches for 1,000 kilometres (600 miles) along the west coast, from Peru into northern Chile. Patagonia, in southern Argentina, is another dry region.

Did you know?

Every few years, a current of warm water flows southwards along the west coast of South America. This current is called El Niño. It causes unusual weather, such as storms, heavy rain, floods, and droughts. This weather not only happens in South America, but in many other parts of the world.

WHAT PLANTS AND ANIMALS LIVE IN SOUTH AMERICA?

An amazing number of plants and animals live in South America. Some of them are so unusual that they are not found in any other part of the world.

Flowering plants

Thousands of types of flowering plants live in the Amazon rainforest, including beautiful orchids. Many orchids live high up on the tree branches. Their roots dangle down and collect water from the air.

The rainforest is not the only place to find unusual plants. A very rare plant called the *Puya raimondii* grows in the Andes in Peru. The plant only flowers once in its life, when it is about 100 years old. It dies shortly afterwards.

This map shows where different kinds of plants grow in South America.

North Atlantic Ocean

Equator

Galapagos Islands

Andes

Amazon

Brazilian Highlands

Pacific Ocean

Atacama Desert

Andes

Gran Chaco

Pampas

Patagonia

South Atlantic Ocean

N
W ⊕ E
S

Tropical rainforest
Tropical thorn forest
Temperate rainforest
Evergreen trees and shrubs
Grassland and savannah
Steppe and scrub
Desert
Alpine and high plateau

Falkland Islands

South Georgia

0   800 miles
0   1000 km

The plants of the pampas have **adapted** to the warm, dry conditions in Argentina.

Grassland plants

Pampas grass grows quickly in spring before the weather gets too hot and dry. It grows in large clumps, up to 4 metres (13 feet) tall and has very long roots for sucking up water from deep underground. The pampas is so hot and dry that fires often break out. Many plants cannot survive fire but grasses are able to grow back from their underground roots.

Did you know?

The Atacama Desert in Chile is so dry that very few plants can live there. One plant that has adapted to the harsh conditions is the Copiapoa cactus. It grows in low, bushy clumps close to the coast. This tough plant copes with the lack of rain by getting all the water it needs from the thick fogs which roll in off the sea. It soaks up the fog through its leaves.

Life on the pampas

Some animals have adapted to life on the pampas. Rheas are large birds. They cannot fly but use their long legs to run at speeds of more than 50 kilometres (31 miles) per hour. Cavies are **mammals**, related to guinea pigs. Like many pampas animals, they live in **burrows** to protect themselves from fires. Giant anteaters are also mammals. They use smell to find a termites' mound or ants' nest. Then they break it open with their huge, curved claws. They lick up the termites or ants with their long, sticky tongues.

Rainforest animals

A huge number of animals live in the rainforests of South America. A single tree may be home to some 1,500 types of insect alone. Many animals live in the treetops where there are plenty of leaves, flowers, and fruit to eat. Apart from insects, there are also monkeys, frogs, tree snakes, and birds, such as toucans and macaws. Lower down, jaguars roam the gloomy forest floor, hunting for rodents, deer, and birds to eat.

The anaconda is one of the animals that lives in the rainforests of Venezuela.

Andean condors feed on dead animals that they spot from high up in the air.

Animals of the mountains

It is freezing cold and windy in the Andes. Even so, many animals live high up in the mountains. Some animals, like alpacas and chinchillas, have thick, shaggy coats to keep them warm. Andean condors use their huge wings to glide above the mountains.

WILDLIFE IN DANGER

Tens of thousands of South American plants and animals are in danger of dying out because their **habitats** are being destroyed by humans.

● *Plants*	● *Mammals*	● *Birds*	● *Insects*
Alerce cypress	Giant otter	Andean condor	Morpho butterfly
Aniba rosewood	Golden lion tamarin	Blue-throated	
Brazilian walnut	Jaguar	macaw	
Monkey puzzle tree	Spectacled bear	Harpy eagle	
Tulipwood tree	Uakari	Hyacinth macaw	
		Spix's macaw	

WHAT ARE SOUTH AMERICA'S NATURAL RESOURCES?

South America has many **natural resources**. It also has a lot of rich farmland. Many South American countries have not used their resources and are quite poor. The poorest countries are Bolivia and Guyana. The richest countries are Argentina, Brazil, and Chile. They have used their resources to build up many businesses and industries.

Did you know?

The **currency** used in Venezuela is called the bolivar. It is named after a South American general, Simon Bolivar (1783–1830). He spent his life fighting to free South America from Spanish rule (see page 20). He won freedom not only for his own country, Venezuela, but also for Bolivia, Colombia, Ecuador, and Peru.

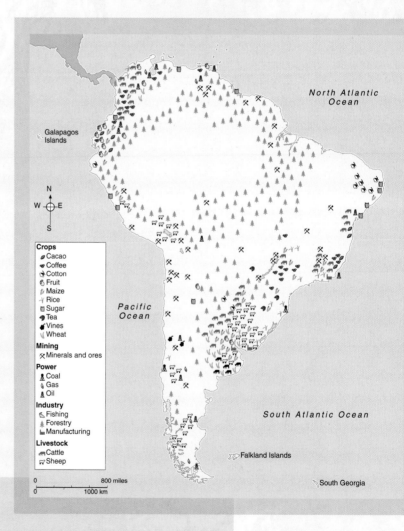

This map shows how South America's natural resources are distributed across the continent.

Mining and minerals

South America has huge amounts of precious **minerals**. Lots of oil comes from Venezuela. Oil is also found in Argentina, Brazil, Colombia, Ecuador, and Peru. There are tin mines in Bolivia and Brazil. Chile produces large quantities of copper and **iron ore**, coal, gold, and silver. Bauxite, which is used to make the metal aluminium, is mined in Guyana and Surinam. Colombia has valuable coal mines and also produces over half of the world's emeralds.

Important industries

Factories in Argentina make steel, chemicals, machinery, and electrical equipment. Brazil is the continent's leading producer of cars, aircraft, iron, and **textiles**. Textiles are also made in Uruguay. In some parts of the continent, **native** South American people make traditional handicrafts to sell. These goods are made by hand or in factories.

Emeralds mined in Columbia are some of South America's most valuable natural resources.

17

Crops, such as bananas, coffee, and sugar-cane, are grown on huge farms called **plantations**.

Farming

About a third of the land in South America is used for farming. Most farms are small plots of land and farmers struggle to grow enough food for their families. But South America also has some of the largest farms in the world. Sheep and cattle are kept on huge farms called ranches.

Forestry and fishing

Many valuable products come from Brazil's rainforests. They include wood from rosewood and mahogany trees, which is used to make furniture and other goods. Other forest products include Brazil nuts, dates, coconuts, palm oil, and medicines made from forest plants.

Fishing is also important in South America, especially along the Pacific (west) coast. Chile and Peru have the largest fishing industries. Their fishing fleets catch huge quantities of anchovies and sardines.

WHAT COUNTRIES AND CITIES ARE IN SOUTH AMERICA?

South America is divided into twelve countries and two other small **territories**. The territories are French Guiana and the Falkland Islands. Brazil is the largest country in South America and the fifth largest country in the world. It is about fifty times bigger than Surinam, which is the smallest country in the continent.

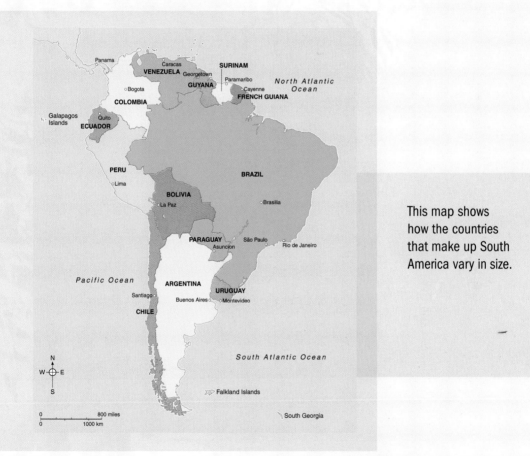

This map shows how the countries that make up South America vary in size.

COUNTRY AND CITY FACTS

Biggest country: Brazil – 8,547,404 square km (3,300,171 square miles)

Smallest country: Surinam – 163,265 square km (63,037 square miles)

Biggest city (by population): São Paulo – 18 million people

Highest capital city: La Paz, Bolivia – 3,660 metres (12,007 ft) above sea level

South American history

In the early 1500s, Europeans began to settle in South America. Spain ruled most of the continent. Brazil was ruled by Portugal. The Europeans often behaved very cruelly towards the native peoples. They destroyed the ancient Inca civilization, and forced people to speak their languages and to follow their religion of Christianity. European rule lasted until the 1800s. Then most of the South American countries fought for and gained their freedom.

The Spanish explorers that arrived in South America were known as the *conquistadors*.

Government and politics

Today, the twelve countries of South America are all **independent republics**. They are ruled by **presidents** and governments which have been elected by the people. However, the territories of French Guiana and the Falkland Islands still belong to France and Britain.

São Paulo is the second biggest city in the world and Brazil's main business centre.

Crowded cities

More than three-quarters of South America's people live in cities. Millions of poor people have moved from the countryside into the cities to search for work. The biggest cities are São Paulo in Brazil (18 million people) and Buenos Aires in Argentina (14 million people). Brazil's capital city is Brasilia. Buenos Aires is the capital of Argentina and the country's major port. About 40 per cent of Argentinians live in or near the city.

Did you know?

The Pan-American Highway is a series of connecting roads that link the countries of South America, Central America, and the United States. The Highway begins in Alaska in the United States and stretches for nearly 25,000 kilometres (15,534 miles) right the way down to Chile. It crosses the borders of 13 countries and passes through every type of landscape from thick rainforest to high mountains.

WHO LIVES IN SOUTH AMERICA?

During the 1900s, the population of South America grew very quickly. Today, about 380 million people live on the continent. That is about 6 per cent of the world's population. Some parts of South America are very crowded, especially the big cities. But places such as the Atacama Desert and Amazon rainforest have very few people living there.

POPULATION FIGURES

This chart shows the percentage of South America's population that lives in each country:

- Brazil (50%)
- Colombia (11%)
- Argentina (10%)
- Peru (8%)
- Venezuela (7%)
- Chile (4%)
- Ecuador (4%)
- Bolivia (2.5%)
- Paraguay (2%)
- Uruguay (1%)
- Guyana, Surinam, and French Guiana (0.5%)

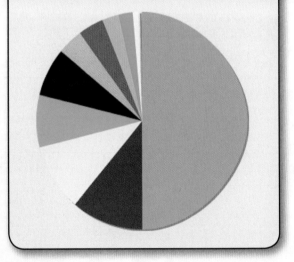

In most countries, the largest group of people are called *mestizos*. They are people of mixed European and native South American descent.

People of South America

Before the Europeans arrived, the South American continent was home to many native people. Large numbers were killed by the European settlers or by diseases that the Europeans brought with them. Today, native South Americans make up only about two per cent of the population. The next largest group of people is descended from African slaves. They were brought by the Europeans to work in South America and the Caribbean.

The Inca people keep their culture, music, and traditions alive today.

Did you know?

The Inca people ruled large parts of South America from the 1100s. Their **empire** was based around the Andes and included parts of modern-day Argentina, Bolivia, Chile, Ecuador, and Peru. In 1532, Spanish soldiers arrived in the empire, greedy for Inca gold. They killed the Inca emperor and set about destroying the empire.

South American languages

Most South Americans speak Spanish. People speak Portuguese in Brazil, French in French Guiana, Dutch in Surinam, and English, Hindi, and Urdu in Guyana. Many ancient South American languages are also spoken. The most common is Quechua, which was the language of the Incas. It is spoken by about 14 million people in Argentina, Bolivia, Chile, Colombia, Ecuador, and Peru.

Rich and poor

There are wealthy people in every South American country. They may be landowners, business people, or military and political leaders. But most South Americans are poor. Many poor people have moved from the countryside to the big cities, hoping to make a better life for their families. However, many end up living in **slums** on the edge of the city.

In the city slums, people live in very poor conditions, with tin houses and no running water, toilets, or electricity.

Rainforest people

Millions of native people once lived in South America's rainforests. Traditionally, they grew crops and hunted animals for food. They treated the forest with great care because they relied on it to keep them alive. Today, there are fewer than 200,000 rainforest people left and their future is under threat because large patches of rainforest are being cut down.

The rainforest people still try to live in harmony with the forest and carry out their traditional rituals.

Religion in South America

The Europeans who came to South America in the 1500s brought their Christian religion with them. They forced native people to give up their own gods and beliefs. Today, most people in South America are Christian, and belong to the Roman Catholic Church.

WHAT FAMOUS PLACES ARE IN SOUTH AMERICA?

Ancient landmarks

Many ancient Inca ruins have been found in South America. The most famous are those of Machu Picchu, perched high up in the Andes in Peru. Machu Picchu was an important Inca city between 1400 and 1500.

At Nazca in southern Peru the desert floor is covered with enormous drawings of animals and gods. The drawings may have been part of a gigantic calendar marked out about 2,300 years ago.

This map shows some of the famous landmarks that can be found across the South American continent.

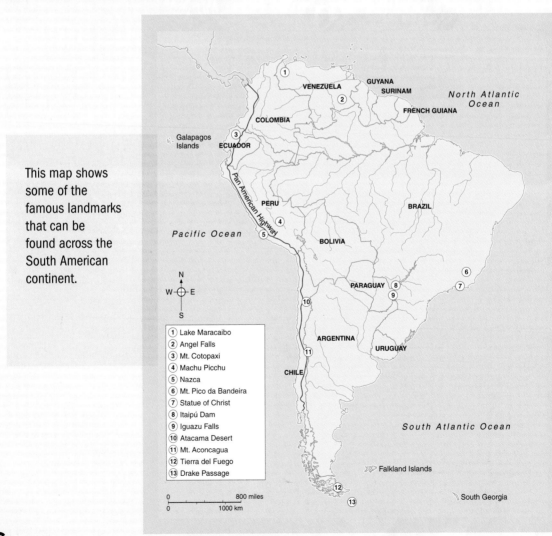

1. Lake Maracaibo
2. Angel Falls
3. Mt. Cotopaxi
4. Machu Picchu
5. Nazca
6. Mt. Pico da Bandeira
7. Statue of Christ
8. Itaipú Dam
9. Iguazu Falls
10. Atacama Desert
11. Mt. Aconcagua
12. Tierra del Fuego
13. Drake Passage

The statue's arms are spread wide open to welcome the world.

Modern landmarks

South America has many modern landmarks. One of the most famous is the huge statue of Jesus Christ which stands on top of Corcovado Mountain overlooking the city of Rio de Janeiro, Brazil.

Another striking building is the Itaipú Dam on the River Parana in Paraguay. It was finished in 1991. It is one of the world's biggest dams and produces lots of **hydro-electricity**.

Natural wonders

As well as the Angel Falls, South America also has the Iguazu Falls on the border between Argentina and Brazil. The falls are 82 metres (269 feet) high and 3 kilometres (2 miles) wide.

South America is also famous for its many volcanoes. Cotopaxi is 5,897 metres (19,347 feet) high and is one of the highest volcanoes in the world. It stands in the Andes near Quito in Ecuador and last erupted in the early 1900s.

CONTINENTS COMPARISON CHART

Continent	Area	Population	
AFRICA	30,365,000 square kilometres (11,720,000 square miles)	906 million	
ANTARCTICA	14,200,000 square kilometres (5,500,000 square miles)	officially none, but about 4,000 people live on the research stations during the summer and over 3,000 people visit as tourists each year. People have lived there for as long as three and a half years at a time.	
ASIA	44,614,000 square kilometres (17,226,200 square miles)	almost 4,000 million	
AUSTRALIA	7,713,364 square kilometres (2,966,136 square miles)	approximately 20,090,400 (2005 estimate)	
EUROPE	10,400,000 square kilometres (4,000,000 square miles)	approximately 727 million (2005 estimate)	
NORTH AMERICA	24,230,000 square kilometres (9,355,000 square miles)	approximately 509,915,000 (2005 estimate)	
SOUTH AMERICA	17,814,000 square kilometres (6,878,000 square miles)	380 million	

Number of Countries	Highest Point	Longest River
54 (includes Western Sahara)	Mount Kilimanjaro, Tanzania — 5,895 metres (19,340 feet)	Nile River — 6,695 kilometres (4,160 miles)
none, but over 23 countries have research stations in Antarctica	Vinson Massif — 4,897 metres (16,067 feet)	River Onyx — 12 kilometres (7.5 miles) **Biggest Ice Shelf** Ross Ice Shelf in western Antarctica — 965 kilometres (600 miles) long.
50	Mount Everest, Tibet and Nepal — 8,850 metres (29,035 feet)	Yangtze River, China — 6,300 kilometres (3,914 miles)
1	Mount Kosciusko — 2,229 metres (7,313 feet)	Murray River — 2,520 kilometres (1,566 miles)
47	Mount Elbrus, Russia — 5,642 metres (18,510 feet)	River Volga — 3,685 kilometres (2,290 miles)
23	Mount McKinley (Denali) in Alaska — 6,194 metres (20,320 feet)	Mississippi/Missouri River System — 6,270 kilometres (3,895 miles)
12	Aconcagua, Argentina — 6,959 metres (22,834 feet)	Amazon River — 6,400 kilometres (4,000 miles)

GLOSSARY

adapted when plants or animals have special features to help them live in a place

burrow underground hole lived in by an animal

climate weather a place usually has over a long time

crust rocky surface of the Earth

currency the money used in a country

current river of hot or cold water running through the sea

drought long period of unusually dry weather

empire group of countries ruled by a single person or government

equator imaginary line around the middle of the Earth

eruption to throw out hot ash and rock

habitat where something lives

hydro-electricity electricity produced from the power of running water

independent country which rules itself

iron ore rocks which contain the metal iron

isthmus narrow strip of land

maize grain crop also called corn

mammal animal that has hair and feeds its babies on milk

mineral coal, gemstones, metals, and so on, that are mined from the Earth

native original people, animal, or plants of an area

natural resource country's stock of oil, coal, metals, and so on

pampas very large, grassy plains with no trees

plantation large area used for growing a crop

president elected head of government in a republic

republic country governed by a president

slum poor and overcrowded part of a city

territory land, such as islands or large cities, which belong to a country far away

textiles fabrics and materials

FURTHER INFORMATION

Books

All About Continents: North & South America, Bruce McClish (Heinemann Library, 2004)

Continents: South America, Mary Fox (Heinemann Library, 2002)

Destination Detectives: Brazil, Ali Brownlie Bojang (Raintree, 2006)

We're From Brazil, Emma Lynch (Heinemann Library, 2005)

Useful websites

- Lots of facts, figures, statistics, and maps about the world's continents, countries, cities, languages, and people:
  www.worldatlas.com

- Provides details of the latest news and current events from South America:
  www.southamericadaily.com

- Map-based games based on the countries and capital cities of South America:
  www.sheppardsoftware.com/South_America_Geography

Disclaimer

All the internet addresses (URLs) given in this book were valid at the time of going to press. However, due to the dynamic nature of the internet, some addresses may have changed, or sites may have ceased to exist since publication. While the author and publishers regret any inconvenience this may cause readers, no responsibility for such changes can be accepted by either the author(s) or the publishers.

INDEX

Titles in the Exploring Continents series include:

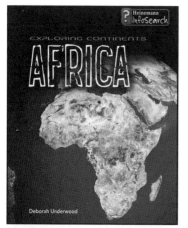

Hardback   0 431 09742 9

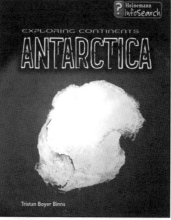

Hardback   0 431 09743 7

Hardback   0 431 09744 5

Hardback   0 431 09745 3

Hardback   0 431 09746 1

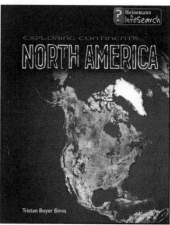

Hardback   0 431 09747 X

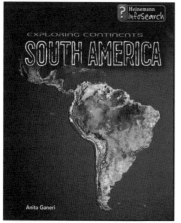

Hardback   0 431 09748 8

Find out about other titles from Heinemann Library on our website www.heinemann.co.uk/library